Embracing Wellness: A Personal Workbook for Overcoming Health Anxiety

Disclaimer:

This Workbook is for educational purposes only and not a substitute for professional medical or mental health advice. Consult a qualified healthcare professional for diagnosis, treatment, or management of health anxiety. Individual experiences may vary, so consider personal circumstances and consult a healthcare professional before implementing any workbook suggestions. By using this workbook, you acknowledge your responsibility for your well-being, and the creators disclaim liability for any loss or damage from its use.

This Workbook Includes:

Chapter 1: Understanding Health Anxiety
- Definition and common symptoms
- Differentiating between normal concern and health anxiety
- Reflective exercises to help readers assess their own health anxiety levels
- Identifying triggers and patterns

Chapter 2: Changing Thought Patterns
- Introduction to cognitive distortions commonly associated with health anxiety
- Examples and exercises to help identify and challenge distorted thinking
- Strategies for reframing negative thoughts related to health anxiety
- Positive affirmations and self-talk exercises

Chapter 3: Managing Anxiety and Stress
- Breathing exercises, mindfulness, and meditation
- Progressive muscle relaxation and guided imagery
- Strategies for accepting and managing uncertainty in health-related situations
- Developing a balanced approach to seeking medical advice

Chapter 4: Taking Control of Your Health Anxiety
- Identifying sources of support: friends, family, and professional help
- Communicating with loved ones about your health anxiety
- Encouraging readers to set achievable goals related to their health anxiety
- Tracking progress and celebrating milestones

Introduction:

Welcome to the Workbook for Overcoming Health Anxiety!

I applaud your decision to take control of your health anxiety and embark on a journey of self-discovery and growth. This workbook is designed to provide you with the tools, knowledge, and support you need to overcome the challenges associated with health anxiety.

Living with health anxiety can be overwhelming, but it's important to remember that you are not alone. Many others have walked this path before you, and they have come out stronger, more resilient, and more confident in their ability to manage their anxiety. With the right mindset and strategies, you too can reclaim your life from the grip of health anxiety.

Introduce yourself!
Who does this workbook belong to ?

_____

Motivation to Take Control of Your Health Anxiety

It's natural to feel apprehensive about your health from time to time. However, when worries about your well-being consume your every thought, it's essential to take action and regain control. You have the power within you to break free from the chains of health anxiety and experience a life filled with joy, peace, and fulfillment.

Imagine a life where you can trust your body, where you can embrace each day with optimism and confidence. By engaging in the exercises and techniques outlined in this workbook, you will learn to challenge your anxious thoughts, reframe your negative beliefs, and develop a more rational and balanced perspective. You will gain the skills necessary to manage your anxiety effectively and live a life that is not dictated by fear.

Making the Most of this Workbook

To make the most of this workbook, it's important to approach it with an open mind and a commitment to your personal growth. Take the time to engage fully with each exercise, reflect on your thoughts and feelings, and be honest with yourself. This workbook is your companion on the path to healing, and it will guide you step-by-step toward a healthier and happier you.

The workbook is structured to provide a comprehensive understanding of health anxiety while offering practical strategies to help you manage and overcome it.

Remember, progress may not always be linear, and it's okay to have setbacks along the way. Be patient and kind to yourself as you navigate this journey. You have already taken the first step by opening this workbook, and I believe in your ability to transform your relationship with health anxiety.

By working through the chapters and exercises in this workbook, you are empowering yourself to take control of your mental well-being. I encourage you to embrace this opportunity for growth, and I am here to support you every step of the way. Together, let's embark on a transformative journey toward a life free from the constraints of health anxiety.

Chapter 1: Understanding Health Anxiety

Definition and Symptoms of Health Anxiety

Health anxiety, at its core, involves an intense fear of having an undiagnosed medical condition or the belief that minor symptoms indicate a severe illness. Individuals with health anxiety constantly seek reassurance from medical professionals, engage in excessive checking behaviors, and may frequently visit doctors or undergo medical tests to alleviate their anxiety. They are highly vigilant about any physical sensations or changes in their bodies and tend to interpret them as signs of serious illness.

Common symptoms and behaviors associated with health anxiety include excessive worry and fear of having a specific illness, persistent checking of bodily sensations or medical information, frequent searching for medical information on the internet, and seeking multiple medical opinions. These individuals often experience a high level of distress, which can manifest as frequent panic attacks, difficulty sleeping, irritability, and impaired daily functioning. The anxiety associated with health anxiety can be debilitating, leading to avoidance of certain situations or places that are perceived as potential health risks.

In addition to the psychological symptoms, health anxiety can also manifest in physical symptoms. Individuals may experience various somatic complaints, such as headaches, muscle tension, dizziness, and gastrointestinal problems, as a result of their heightened anxiety. These physical symptoms further reinforce their belief that they have a serious illness, perpetuating the cycle of anxiety.

It is important to note that health anxiety is distinct from genuine medical conditions or legitimate concerns about one's health. While everyone may experience worries about their health from time to time, individuals with health anxiety experience excessive and persistent anxiety that significantly interferes with their daily lives. It is essential to approach health anxiety with empathy and understanding, as the distress experienced by individuals with this condition is real and can have a profound impact on their well-being.

Differentiating between Normal Concern and Health Anxiety

It's important to differentiate between normal concern about one's health and health anxiety. While it is natural to be concerned about our well-being, health anxiety goes beyond normal levels of worry and becomes a persistent, distressing, and irrational fear of having a serious illness. Understanding the differences can help individuals recognize when their concerns have crossed the threshold into health anxiety.

Normal concern about health typically arises in response to specific symptoms or situations and subsides once a cause is identified or a reasonable explanation is given. It is a temporary state of worry that can be managed through self-care or seeking appropriate medical advice. On the other hand, health anxiety tends to be chronic and persistent, with individuals often fixating on worst-case scenarios and experiencing heightened anxiety even in the absence of clear evidence or symptoms.

Differentiating between normal concern and health anxiety involves considering the intensity and duration of the worry, the impact it has on daily life and functioning, and the degree to which it aligns with actual medical evidence. It's important to remember that seeking appropriate medical advice is crucial, but individuals with health anxiety often struggle to find reassurance even after medical evaluations have ruled out serious illnesses.

By understanding the distinction between normal concern and health anxiety, individuals can begin to gain insight into their own patterns of thinking and behavior. This self-awareness is a crucial step towards developing effective strategies for managing and overcoming health anxiety.

Reflective Exercises to Assess Your Health Anxiety Levels

Understanding the extent and impact of your health anxiety is a crucial step in overcoming it. This section provides you with reflective exercises designed to help you assess your own health anxiety levels. By engaging in these exercises with an open and honest mindset, you can gain valuable insights into your thoughts, emotions, and behaviors surrounding health anxiety.

Take a moment to reflect on your experiences. Consider the frequency and intensity of your health-related worries. How often do you find yourself preoccupied with thoughts of illness? Do these worries interfere with your daily life, relationships, or activities?

_____
_____
_____
_____
_____
_____

Through self-reflection, you can begin to identify the patterns and tendencies that contribute to your health anxiety.

Identifying Triggers and Patterns

Triggers and patterns play a significant role in the development and maintenance of health anxiety. It is essential to identify these triggers and patterns to gain insight into the underlying causes of your health anxiety and to develop effective strategies for managing and overcoming it.

Triggers can be internal or external factors that provoke or worsen your health anxiety. Internal triggers may include specific bodily sensations, such as a racing heart or a headache, while external triggers can be situations, places, or even certain conversations. Reflect on the situations, thoughts, or events that tend to trigger your health anxiety. By identifying these triggers, you can begin to understand the specific circumstances that contribute to your anxiety and develop targeted coping mechanisms.

Patterns refer to recurring thoughts, behaviors, or emotions associated with your health anxiety. For example, do you tend to engage in excessive reassurance-seeking behaviors, such as repeatedly searching for medical information online or seeking frequent medical consultations? Do you notice patterns of catastrophic thinking, where you immediately jump to the worst-case scenario? Identifying these patterns can provide valuable insights into the automatic responses and habits that maintain your health anxiety.

Reflect on three specific instances in the past where your health anxiety was triggered. Describe the situations, thoughts, and emotions you experienced during those moments. Notice any commonalities or patterns among the triggers you identified. Write about your insights and reflections on these triggers.

_____
_____
_____
_____
_____
_____
_____
_____
_____
_____
_____
_____
_____
_____
_____
_____
_____
_____
_____
_____
_____
_____
_____
_____
_____
_____
_____
_____
_____
_____

Make two lists: one for internal triggers and one for external triggers. Write down examples of both types of triggers that tend to provoke or worsen your health anxiety. Reflect on the specific bodily sensations, situations, places, or conversations that contribute to your anxiety. Expand on each trigger, describing your thoughts and emotions associated with it.

Examining How Health Anxiety Affects Relationships, Work, and Daily Functioning

Health anxiety can have a profound impact on various aspects of your life, including relationships, work, and daily functioning. It is crucial to examine these effects to fully understand the toll that health anxiety takes on your overall well-being.

Relationships: Health anxiety can strain relationships with family, friends, and romantic partners. The constant need for reassurance and excessive worry can lead to strained communication, misunderstandings, and frustration. Loved ones may struggle to understand the intense fears and concerns associated with health anxiety, which can create distance and a sense of isolation. Examining the impact on your relationships will help you recognize the importance of addressing your health anxiety for the benefit of yourself and your loved ones.

Work: Health anxiety can significantly affect your performance and satisfaction at work. The constant preoccupation with health concerns can distract you, reduce productivity, and impair concentration. It may also lead to excessive sick leave, avoidance of certain tasks or environments, and difficulty making decisions. By exploring the impact of health anxiety on your work life, you can gain insight into the specific challenges you face and begin to develop strategies for managing anxiety in the workplace.

Daily Functioning: Health anxiety can infiltrate every aspect of your daily life. Simple tasks may become overwhelming as you constantly analyze your body, monitor symptoms, and seek reassurance. It can lead to disruptions in sleep patterns, changes in appetite, and a decline in overall well-being. Examining how health anxiety affects your daily functioning will provide a clearer understanding of the areas where you need support and intervention.

Choose a significant relationship in your life, such as a family member, friend, or romantic partner. Write about how your health anxiety has influenced this relationship. Reflect on any communication challenges, misunderstandings, or strains that have arisen due to your anxiety. Consider the emotions and concerns of the other person involved. This exercise helps you understand the effect of health anxiety on your relationships and encourages empathy.

Focus on your work life and assess how health anxiety has affected your performance, satisfaction, and overall experience at work. Write about specific instances where your anxiety interfered with your ability to concentrate, make decisions, or complete tasks. Consider any missed opportunities or negative consequences resulting from your health anxiety. This activity helps you recognize the impact of anxiety on your professional life and identify areas for improvement.

Create a list of various aspects of your daily life, such as sleep, appetite, self-care, social activities, and leisure time. Write about how health anxiety has affected each of these areas individually. Be honest and detailed about the disruptions or difficulties you've experienced. This exercise helps you identify patterns and gain a comprehensive understanding of how health anxiety permeates your daily functioning.

Chapter 2: Changing Thought Patterns

Introduction to Cognitive Distortions Commonly Associated with Health Anxiety

Cognitive distortions are thought patterns that are inaccurate, negative, and irrational. They are commonly associated with health anxiety and can contribute to the maintenance and exacerbation of anxious feelings. Recognizing these cognitive distortions is an important step in overcoming health anxiety and developing a more balanced and rational mindset.

In this section, we will explore some of the most common cognitive distortions related to health anxiety. By understanding these distortions, you can gain insight into the ways in which your thoughts may be influencing your anxiety levels. Recognizing and challenging these distortions will allow you to replace them with more accurate and realistic thinking patterns.

It is essential to remember that cognitive distortions are automatic and often subconscious. They have become ingrained over time, but with practice and awareness, you can begin to unravel their grip on your thoughts. By identifying these distortions and actively working to challenge them, you can gain a sense of control over your thinking patterns and reduce the impact of health anxiety on your daily life.

Examples and Exercises to Help Identify and Challenge Distorted Thinking

Identifying and challenging cognitive distortions associated with health anxiety is a powerful tool for transforming your mindset and reducing anxiety levels. In this section, you will find examples and exercises to help you recognize and challenge distorted thinking patterns.

One common cognitive distortion related to health anxiety is catastrophizing. This distortion involves jumping to the worst-case scenario and imagining the most severe and unlikely outcomes. For example, a minor headache may lead you to immediately think of a brain tumor. By recognizing this thought pattern, you can challenge it by asking yourself for evidence supporting the catastrophic conclusion and considering more realistic alternative explanations.

Another distortion is called selective attention or filtering. This occurs when you focus solely on information that confirms your fears while disregarding any evidence that contradicts them. For instance, you might pay excessive attention to stories of people with rare medical conditions but dismiss statistics showing how uncommon those conditions are. To challenge this distortion, practice seeking out balanced information and considering alternative perspectives.

Overgeneralization:
Example: You experience a minor physical symptom and immediately assume it is a sign of a serious illness.

Exercise:
Journal of instances where you overgeneralize health symptoms. Write down the specific symptom, the automatic negative thought that arises, and any evidence that supports or contradicts your assumption. Then, challenge the overgeneralization by considering alternative explanations or possibilities.

_____
_____
_____
_____
_____
_____

Mind Reading:
Example: You believe that doctors and medical professionals are withholding information about your health condition, leading to increased anxiety.

Exercise: Write down the instances where you engage in mind reading regarding your health. Identify the specific thoughts or beliefs you have about what others are thinking or hiding from you. Challenge this distortion by examining the evidence for and against your belief, and consider alternative explanations for the behavior of healthcare professionals.

_____
_____
_____
_____
_____
_____

Emotional Reasoning:
Example: You feel anxious and convinced that something is wrong with your health, assuming that your emotions indicate the presence of an illness.

Exercise:
Pay attention to moments when you rely on emotional reasoning to validate health concerns. Write down the situations where your emotions guide your thoughts about your health. Examine the evidence supporting your emotions and consider alternative explanations for your feelings, such as stress or other non-medical factors.

_____
_____
_____
_____
_____
_____

Labeling:
Example: You receive a diagnosis or a medical term related to a symptom, and you immediately define yourself by that condition.

Exercise:
Make a list of times when you label yourself or use negative language to describe your health condition. Write down the specific labels or negative terms you use. Challenge this distortion by considering the limitations of labeling and focusing on the complexities of human health. Reflect on your strengths, achievements, and qualities that extend beyond your health condition.

_____
_____
_____
_____
_____
_____
_____
_____

Strategies for Reframing Negative Thoughts Related to Health Anxiety

Reframing negative thoughts is a powerful technique that can help individuals with health anxiety gain a more balanced and rational perspective. In this section, we will explore strategies to reframe negative thoughts related to health anxiety, allowing you to shift your focus from fear and worry to more positive and constructive thinking patterns.

One effective strategy is to challenge and question your negative thoughts. When a worrisome thought arises, ask yourself for evidence supporting that thought. Often, you will find that your fears are based on assumptions or misinformation rather than actual evidence. By questioning the validity of your negative thoughts, you can begin to replace them with more accurate and realistic ones.

Another strategy is to reframe catastrophic thinking into more balanced and moderate thoughts. For example, if you catch yourself immediately jumping to the worst-case scenario when experiencing a physical symptom, consciously remind yourself that there are various possible explanations for the symptom, and most of them are not life-threatening. By reframing your thoughts, you can create a more balanced and realistic perception of the situation.

Additionally, practicing gratitude can be a powerful way to reframe negative thoughts. Focusing on the positive aspects of your life and expressing gratitude for them can help counterbalance the negative thoughts associated with health anxiety. Incorporating gratitude exercises into your daily routine can shift your mindset towards appreciation and reduce the intensity of anxious thoughts.

Positive Affirmations and Self-Talk Exercises

Positive affirmations and self-talk exercises are valuable tools for challenging negative thoughts and promoting self-empowerment and resilience. In this section, you will explore the power of positive affirmations and learn techniques to incorporate them into your daily life.

Positive affirmations are short, positive statements that you repeat to yourself. They serve as reminders of your strengths, abilities, and capacity for growth. By repeating positive affirmations related to health and well-being, you can counteract negative thoughts and cultivate a more optimistic and confident mindset.

Engaging in self-talk exercises involves consciously monitoring your inner dialogue and transforming negative self-talk into supportive and encouraging statements. For instance, if you catch yourself saying, "I'm always sick," you can reframe it by saying, "I am taking proactive steps to improve my health and well-being." By intentionally changing your self-talk, you can foster a more compassionate and empowering relationship with yourself.

Integrating positive affirmations and self-talk exercises into your daily routine can help rewire your thinking patterns over time. By consistently reinforcing positive and encouraging messages, you are nurturing a mindset that supports your well-being and resilience in the face of health anxiety.

Remember, the process of reframing negative thoughts and incorporating positive affirmations and self-talk exercises requires practice and patience. It is a gradual journey of reshaping your thinking patterns and creating a more supportive inner dialogue. By actively engaging in these strategies, you can reframe your thoughts, cultivate a positive mindset, and empower yourself to overcome health anxiety with confidence and resilience.

Write down positive affirmations related to your health and well-being. Start each entry with a positive affirmation such as "I am resilient," "I am capable of managing my anxiety," or "I am taking steps towards my health goals." Reflect on why each affirmation is meaningful to you and how it relates to your journey of overcoming health anxiety. Read your affirmations aloud or silently to yourself daily, allowing them to uplift and inspire you.

___

___

___

___

___

___

___

___

___

___

___

___

___

___

___

___

___

___

Write down any negative thoughts or self-critical statements related to your health anxiety. Take a moment to examine each thought and identify a more positive and supportive alternative. Rewrite the negative thought using positive and empowering language. For example, if the negative thought is "I'm a hypochondriac," reframe it as "I am proactive about my health and take necessary precautions." Practice this exercise regularly to gradually shift your self-talk towards a more constructive and compassionate mindset.

_____
_____
_____
_____
_____
_____
_____
_____
_____
_____
_____
_____
_____
_____
_____
_____
_____
_____
_____
_____
_____
_____
_____
_____
_____
_____
_____
_____
_____
_____

Introducing Logic and Evidence-Based Reasoning to Combat Irrational Beliefs

Developing rational thinking is a fundamental aspect of overcoming health anxiety. By applying logic and evidence-based reasoning, you can challenge and combat irrational beliefs that contribute to anxiety. In this section, we will explore how to incorporate rational thinking into your mindset to promote a more balanced and realistic perspective.

Logic serves as a powerful tool for analyzing and evaluating the validity of thoughts and beliefs. When faced with anxious thoughts related to health, it is essential to examine the evidence supporting those thoughts. Ask yourself: What evidence do I have to support this belief? Is there any logical basis for my fears? Often, you will find that the evidence is scarce or non-existent, which can help you reframe your thinking and reduce anxiety.

Evidence-based reasoning involves seeking out credible information to inform your beliefs and opinions. Instead of relying solely on assumptions or misinformation, actively search for reliable sources of information related to your health concerns. Consult reputable medical professionals, trustworthy websites, or reliable literature. By basing your beliefs on evidence, you can counteract irrational thinking and cultivate a more informed and balanced perspective.

By introducing logic and evidence-based reasoning, you are equipping yourself with tools to challenge and counteract irrational beliefs associated with health anxiety. Through critical analysis of your thoughts and actively seeking credible information, you can develop a more rational and grounded approach to your health concerns.

Techniques for Questioning Anxious Thoughts and Finding Alternative Perspectives

In addition to logic and evidence-based reasoning, there are specific techniques you can utilize to question anxious thoughts and find alternative perspectives. These techniques are powerful tools for combating irrational beliefs and cultivating a more balanced and realistic mindset.

One effective technique is cognitive restructuring. This involves actively challenging anxious thoughts by asking yourself critical questions. For example, when you notice an anxious thought, ask yourself: What evidence supports this thought? Is there any evidence that contradicts it? What are some alternative explanations or perspectives? By engaging in this process, you can uncover the flaws in your anxious thinking and open yourself up to more rational and balanced viewpoints.

Another technique is reframing. When confronted with anxious thoughts, consciously shift your focus to alternative perspectives. Consider the best-case scenario or more neutral interpretations of the situation. Reframing helps you broaden your perspective and challenge the narrow and negative thinking patterns associated with health anxiety.

Additionally, seeking social support and outside perspectives can be beneficial. Share your concerns with trusted individuals, such as friends, family, or support groups. They can provide alternative viewpoints, offer reassurance, and help you gain new insights into your fears. Engaging in open and honest conversations can challenge and reshape your anxious thoughts, providing a fresh perspective and support along your journey.

By incorporating techniques for questioning anxious thoughts and finding alternative perspectives, you are actively challenging and reshaping the cognitive patterns associated with health anxiety. These techniques empower you to develop a more balanced and rational mindset, allowing you to approach your health concerns with clarity and resilience.

Remember, developing rational thinking takes time and practice. Be patient with yourself as you engage in these techniques. With persistence and an open mind, you can reframe your thinking, challenge irrational beliefs, and cultivate a more rational and balanced approach to health anxiety.

Cognitive Restructuring:

- Identify an anxious thought related to health anxiety, such as "I'm convinced I have a serious illness."
- Ask yourself: What evidence supports this thought? Are there any objective facts or test results indicating a serious illness?
- Consider if there is any evidence that contradicts this thought, such as previous medical check-ups that showed no abnormalities.
- Generate alternative explanations or perspectives, such as "It could be a minor health issue or a symptom related to stress."
- Reflect on the flaws in your anxious thinking and try to adopt a more rational and balanced viewpoint based on the evidence.

Reframing:

- When you catch yourself having an anxious thought about your health, consciously shift your focus to alternative perspectives.
- Consider the best-case scenario: "There's a higher chance that this symptom is benign rather than a serious health condition."
- Think of more neutral interpretations: "It's normal to experience occasional physical discomfort, and it doesn't automatically mean something is seriously wrong."
- Remind yourself that your current perspective may be influenced by anxiety, and intentionally broaden your outlook to challenge negative thinking patterns.

Seeking Social Support:

- Reach out to a trusted friend or family member and share your health concerns.
- Explain your anxious thoughts and fears, allowing them to provide alternative viewpoints and perspectives.
- Listen to their reassurance and insights, taking note of any rational arguments they present.
- Engage in open and honest conversations about your health anxiety to challenge and reshape your thinking.
- Consider joining a support group where individuals with similar experiences can offer additional perspectives and support.

Anxious Thought Analysis:

Take a few minutes to reflect on a recent anxious thought related to health anxiety that you've had. Write down the following:

- Describe the specific anxious thought in detail.
- What triggered this thought? Was there a specific event or symptom that led to it?
- List the evidence that supports this anxious thought.
- Identify any evidence that contradicts or challenges this thought.
- Brainstorm alternative explanations or perspectives that could provide a more balanced view.
- Reflect on the flaws in your anxious thinking and explore how you can adopt a more rational perspective.

Reframing Exercise:
Choose a common anxious thought related to health anxiety and reframe it in writing. For example:

- Original anxious thought: "Every ache or pain is a sign of a serious illness."
- Reframed perspective: "Occasional aches and pains are a normal part of being human and usually not indicative of a serious health issue. Most of the time, these sensations resolve on their own."
- Write a paragraph or two explaining your reframed perspective. Focus on incorporating rational, evidence-based arguments and alternative viewpoints. Aim to broaden your perspective and challenge the narrow and negative thinking patterns associated with health anxiety.

Chapter 3: Managing Anxiety and Stress

Breathing Exercises, Mindfulness, and Meditation

Relaxation techniques such as breathing exercises, mindfulness, and meditation are powerful tools for managing and reducing anxiety associated with health anxiety. In this section, we will explore these techniques and how they can bring about a sense of calm and balance in your life.

Breathing exercises are simple yet effective techniques that can help regulate your nervous system and induce relaxation. By focusing on your breath, you can shift your attention away from anxious thoughts and bring your mind into the present moment. Deep, diaphragmatic breathing slows down your heart rate, decreases muscle tension, and activates the body's relaxation response. Incorporating regular breathing exercises into your daily routine can help you build resilience and manage anxiety more effectively.

Mindfulness involves bringing your awareness to the present moment without judgment. By observing your thoughts, emotions, and bodily sensations with curiosity and acceptance, you can cultivate a sense of inner calm and detachment from anxious thoughts related to health. Mindfulness practices can include mindful breathing, body scans, and mindful eating. Engaging in mindfulness exercises can help you develop a non-reactive stance toward your health anxiety and reduce the distress associated with it.

Meditation is a practice that involves focusing your attention and eliminating the stream of thoughts that often consume our minds. Through regular meditation, you can cultivate a state of deep relaxation and inner peace. Meditation techniques can include guided meditations, mantra repetition, or simply sitting in silence and observing your thoughts. By incorporating meditation into your routine, you can enhance self-awareness, reduce stress, and develop a more resilient mindset.

By engaging in these relaxation techniques, you are taking an active role in managing your health anxiety and promoting overall well-being. As you practice breathing exercises, mindfulness, and meditation, remember that consistency and patience are key. Over time, these techniques can help you build a solid foundation of relaxation, resilience, and emotional balance.

Breathing Exercises:

- Find a quiet and comfortable place to sit or lie down.
- Close your eyes and take a few deep breaths, inhaling through your nose and exhaling through your mouth.
- Focus your attention on your breath. Notice the sensation of the air entering and leaving your body.

- Gradually lengthen your inhalations and exhalations, aiming for slow, deep breaths.
- As you breathe, imagine tension and anxiety leaving your body with each exhale.
- Practice this breathing exercise for a few minutes each day, gradually increasing the duration as you become more comfortable.

Mindfulness:

- Choose an everyday activity, such as eating a meal or taking a shower, to practice mindfulness.
- Bring your full attention to the present moment as you engage in the chosen activity.
- Notice the physical sensations, smells, tastes, and textures associated with the activity.
- Whenever your mind wanders to anxious thoughts, gently guide your attention back to the present moment and the task at hand.
- Avoid judging or analyzing your thoughts and experiences. Instead, observe them with curiosity and acceptance.
- Start with short periods of mindfulness practice and gradually extend the duration as you feel more at ease with the process.

Meditation:

- Find a quiet and comfortable space where you can sit or lie down without distractions.
- Choose a meditation technique that resonates with you, such as guided meditation, mantra repetition, or silent meditation.
- Set a timer for your desired meditation duration, starting with a few minutes and gradually increasing the time as you progress.
- Close your eyes, relax your body, and focus your attention on your chosen meditation object (e.g., breath, mantra, or body sensations).
- Whenever your mind wanders, gently redirect your attention back to the chosen object without judgment.
- Practice regularly, ideally at the same time each day, to develop a consistent meditation routine.

Remember, these practices require patience and persistence. Start with small increments of time and gradually increase your practice duration. Consider incorporating these techniques into your daily routine and experimenting with different approaches to find what works best for you. As you engage in breathing exercises, mindfulness, and meditation, you will cultivate a greater sense of relaxation, resilience, and emotional balance.

Progressive Muscle Relaxation and Guided Imagery

Progressive muscle relaxation and guided imagery are additional relaxation techniques that can significantly reduce anxiety and promote a sense of calm and well-being. Let's explore how these techniques can be applied to managing health anxiety.

Progressive muscle relaxation involves systematically tensing and relaxing different muscle groups in your body. By bringing awareness to the sensations of tension and then consciously releasing it, you can promote deep physical relaxation and relieve muscle tension associated with anxiety. Regular practice of progressive muscle relaxation can help you become more attuned to your body's response to stress and anxiety, allowing you to intervene and alleviate tension as needed.

Guided imagery is a technique that involves using your imagination to create calming mental images or scenes. Through guided imagery exercises, you can transport your mind to a peaceful and serene place, allowing you to temporarily escape from anxious thoughts and emotions. By engaging your senses and vividly imagining a soothing environment, you can activate the relaxation response and reduce the physiological symptoms of anxiety.

Both progressive muscle relaxation and guided imagery can be practiced individually or with the guidance of recordings or apps specifically designed for relaxation purposes. You can explore various resources to find guided sessions that resonate with you and fit your personal preferences.

Incorporating progressive muscle relaxation and guided imagery into your daily routine offers you a toolkit of relaxation techniques to draw from whenever you feel overwhelmed by health anxiety. By regularly practicing these techniques, you can cultivate a greater sense of inner peace, physical relaxation, and emotional well-being.

Progressive Muscle Relaxation:

- Find a quiet and comfortable space where you can sit or lie down.
- Close your eyes and take a few deep breaths to center yourself.
- Start with your toes and consciously tense the muscles in that area for a few seconds, then release the tension completely, feeling the relaxation.
- Gradually work your way up through different muscle groups, such as your calves, thighs, abdomen, shoulders, neck, and face.
- As you tense and relax each muscle group, pay attention to the sensations and the contrast between tension and relaxation.
- Take your time and continue the process until you have systematically relaxed each muscle group in your body.

Guided Imagery:

- Find a quiet and comfortable space where you can sit or lie down.
- Close your eyes and take a few deep breaths to relax.
- Choose a guided imagery resource, such as a recording or an app, that provides calming and soothing imagery.
- Follow the instructions provided, which may involve imagining a peaceful scene in nature, visualizing specific details like colors, sounds, and textures.
- Engage your senses and immerse yourself in the imagined environment, allowing yourself to feel the relaxation and tranquility.
- Let go of any anxious thoughts and fully embrace the positive sensations and emotions associated with the guided imagery.

Strategies for Accepting and Managing Uncertainty in Health-Related Situations

Dealing with uncertainty can be challenging, especially when it comes to health anxiety. It's natural to feel anxious and overwhelmed when faced with the unknown. However, there are strategies you can use to help accept and manage uncertainty in health-related situations, allowing you to navigate life with resilience and peace of mind.

One powerful strategy is to practice mindfulness and stay present. When uncertainty arises, try to focus on the present moment rather than worrying about the future or dwelling on the past. By grounding yourself in the here and now, you can redirect your attention away from anxious thoughts and find a sense of calm. Engaging in mindfulness exercises, such as deep breathing or body scans, can help you accept the present moment and reduce distress associated with uncertainty.

Another effective strategy is reframing uncertainty as an opportunity for growth and adaptation. Instead of seeing uncertainty as something to fear, view it as a natural part of life that presents learning and personal development opportunities. Embrace the idea that uncertainty can help you build resilience, flexibility, and problem-solving skills. Shifting your mindset in this way can empower you to approach uncertainty with curiosity and confidence.

In addition, building a support system is crucial when coping with uncertainty. Surround yourself with trusted friends, family, or support groups who can provide understanding, encouragement, and guidance. Sharing your fears and concerns with others who empathize with your experiences can offer new perspectives and help you feel supported during times of uncertainty.

Write down a recent health-related situation that triggered uncertainty or anxiety for you. Describe in detail how you typically react to uncertainty. What thoughts and emotions arise? How does it affect your well-being?

Identify a specific health-related uncertainty or fear that you often struggle with. Write down your initial thoughts and beliefs about this uncertainty, acknowledging any negative or anxious perspectives. Now, challenge those thoughts and beliefs by reframing the uncertainty as an opportunity for growth and adaptation. Write a paragraph or two exploring how this reframed perspective can empower you to approach uncertainty with curiosity, confidence, and a focus on personal development.

Write down the names of individuals in your life whom you trust and can turn to for understanding, encouragement, and guidance during uncertain times. For each person, describe why they are an important part of your support system and how their support can help you navigate health-related uncertainties.

_____
_____
_____
_____
_____
_____
_____
_____
_____
_____
_____
_____
_____
_____
_____
_____
_____
_____
_____
_____
_____
_____
_____
_____
_____
_____
_____
_____
_____
_____
_____
_____
_____
_____
_____

Developing a Balanced Approach to Seeking Medical Advice

Seeking medical advice can be both helpful and challenging for individuals with health anxiety. While seeking reassurance can provide temporary relief from anxiety, it can also perpetuate dependence and reinforce anxious thoughts. Developing a balanced approach to seeking medical advice is essential in effectively managing health anxiety.

One important aspect of finding balance is recognizing the difference between appropriate and excessive reassurance-seeking behaviors. It's natural to seek medical advice when experiencing health concerns, but it's important to be mindful of when seeking reassurance becomes compulsive and reinforces anxious thoughts. Take time to reflect on your patterns of seeking medical advice and evaluate whether your actions align with reasonable health concerns or are primarily driven by anxiety.

Establishing open and honest communication with your healthcare provider is another key component of a balanced approach. Share your concerns, fears, and anxieties with your healthcare provider in a collaborative manner. Building a trusting relationship allows you to work together in developing a personalized healthcare plan that addresses your needs while also considering the potential impact of health anxiety. Engaging in conversations with your provider about appropriate check-ins, tests, and treatments ensures that your medical care aligns with your specific circumstances.

Furthermore, integrating self-empowerment strategies alongside seeking medical advice can contribute to a balanced approach. Engage in relaxation techniques, cognitive restructuring, and self-care activities that help you manage anxiety independently. By developing a repertoire of self-help tools, you can take an active role in managing your health anxiety while still receiving necessary medical support.

By adopting a balanced approach to seeking medical advice, you can strike a harmonious balance between proactive health management and avoiding excessive dependence. This empowers you to make informed decisions, advocate for your needs, and navigate health-related situations with a greater sense of control and confidence.

Stress Management

Stress management plays a crucial role in overcoming health anxiety. Identifying your stressors and developing a personalized stress management plan can help you regain a sense of control and reduce anxiety in your life. In this section, we will explore strategies to help you identify stressors and create an effective stress management plan tailored to your needs.

The first step is to become aware of your stressors. Take some time to reflect on the situations, events, or thoughts that trigger stress in your life. Common stressors for individuals with health anxiety may include medical appointments, health-related news, or even certain bodily sensations. By identifying these triggers, you can gain insight into the specific areas that contribute to your stress and anxiety.

Once you have identified your stressors, you can develop a personalized stress management plan. Start by considering activities or practices that help you relax and alleviate stress. This may include exercise, hobbies, spending time in nature, or engaging in creative outlets. Experiment with different techniques to discover what works best for you.

In addition to relaxation activities, it's important to incorporate healthy coping mechanisms into your stress management plan. This can involve practicing self-care, setting boundaries, and engaging in positive social connections. Make time for activities that bring you joy and nourish your well-being. Prioritize self-care practices such as getting enough sleep, eating a balanced diet, and practicing mindfulness. Building a support system of friends, family, or support groups can provide emotional support and understanding.

Stress Journaling:

- Write about situations, events, or thoughts that triggered stress or anxiety for you during the day.
- Reflect on how these stressors affected your mood, physical sensations, and overall well-being.
- Consider any patterns or common themes that emerge from your journal entries.

_____
_____
_____
_____
_____
_____

Self-Reflection and Mind Mapping:

- Begin branching out from the center, writing down different categories or aspects of your life that may contribute to stress (e.g., work, relationships, health).
- Under each category, identify specific stressors or triggers that come to mind.
- Reflect on how each stressor impacts you and note any associated thoughts or emotions.
- This visual representation can help you see the big picture and identify areas where stress management strategies may be beneficial.

Self-Care Activities and Healthy Coping Mechanisms

Self-care activities and healthy coping mechanisms are essential components of stress management and overall well-being. Incorporating these practices into your daily life can help you reduce anxiety, recharge your energy, and improve your overall resilience. In this section, we will explore various self-care activities and coping mechanisms that can support your journey of overcoming health anxiety.

Self-care activities can take many forms, and it's important to find what resonates with you. Engage in activities that bring you joy, relaxation, and a sense of fulfillment. This may include practicing mindfulness or meditation, taking soothing baths, enjoying nature walks, or pursuing creative outlets such as painting, writing, or playing music. Find activities that help you unwind, recharge, and nurture your emotional well-being.

In addition to self-care activities, it's crucial to develop healthy coping mechanisms that support stress management. Healthy coping mechanisms are strategies you can use to navigate difficult situations and emotions without resorting to unhealthy behaviors or thought patterns. Examples of healthy coping mechanisms include deep breathing exercises, journaling, practicing gratitude, and engaging in physical activity. These techniques can help you regulate your emotions, gain perspective, and reduce anxiety during challenging times.

Building a routine that incorporates self-care and healthy coping mechanisms is key. Consider creating a schedule that includes dedicated time for activities that support your well-being. Be intentional about setting boundaries and prioritizing self-care, even during busy or stressful periods. Remember, self-care is not selfish; it is essential for maintaining your mental and emotional health.

As you explore self-care activities and healthy coping mechanisms, keep in mind that everyone's needs and preferences are unique. Experiment with different practices and find what works best for you. Embrace a holistic approach to self-care, addressing your physical, emotional, and spiritual well-being.

By incorporating self-care activities and healthy coping mechanisms into your life, you can effectively manage stress, reduce anxiety, and cultivate a greater sense of well-being. Remember, self-care is an ongoing practice that requires consistency and self-compassion. Embrace these activities as essential investments in your overall health and happiness.

Chapter 4: Taking Control of Your Health Anxiety

Identifying Sources of Support: Friends, Family, and Professional Help

Building a support system is crucial when it comes to overcoming health anxiety. Having a network of supportive individuals can provide comfort, understanding, and encouragement along your journey. In this section, we will explore the importance of identifying sources of support, including friends, family, and professional help.

First and foremost, consider the people in your life who can offer emotional support and understanding. Friends can play a vital role in providing a listening ear, offering reassurance, and empathizing with your experiences. Reach out to friends whom you trust and feel comfortable sharing your health anxiety struggles with. Cultivate open and honest conversations, allowing them to gain insight into your experiences and provide support when you need it.

Family members can also be a significant source of support. They often have a deeper understanding of your background, history, and personal challenges. Communicate your health anxiety journey with your family members, helping them understand your concerns and providing them with an opportunity to support you. Sharing your experiences can foster a sense of togetherness and create an environment where you feel safe and supported.

Additionally, seeking professional help can be instrumental in managing health anxiety. Mental health professionals, such as therapists or counselors, are trained to provide guidance, support, and evidence-based strategies to help you navigate your health anxiety. They can help you develop coping mechanisms, challenge irrational thoughts, and provide a safe space for you to express your concerns. Consider reaching out to a qualified professional who specializes in anxiety or cognitive-behavioral therapy to provide you with the specific support you need.

Remember, building a support system takes time and effort. Be patient with yourself as you identify and reach out to sources of support. Cultivating these relationships requires open communication, vulnerability, and mutual understanding. Surrounding yourself with individuals who genuinely care about your well-being can provide immense comfort and encouragement as you work towards overcoming health anxiety.

Communicating with Loved Ones about Your Health Anxiety

Effective communication plays a vital role in building a strong support system when it comes to health anxiety. Opening up to your loved ones about your experiences can deepen your connections, foster understanding, and provide the support you need. In this section, we will explore strategies for communicating with your loved ones about your health anxiety.

Start by choosing a time and place where you feel comfortable and can have an uninterrupted conversation. Begin by expressing your desire to share something important and personal. Let your loved ones know that you trust and value their support. Assure them that you are sharing your health anxiety struggles with them because you believe their understanding and support can make a positive difference in your life.

Be open and honest about your experiences with health anxiety. Share how it impacts your daily life, your emotions, and your well-being. Help them understand the specific fears and worries you face and how they affect your thoughts and behaviors. This transparency can create a foundation of empathy and support within your relationships.

It's essential to communicate your needs and boundaries clearly. Let your loved ones know how they can best support you. This may include simply listening without judgment, offering words of encouragement, or helping you engage in activities that promote relaxation and well-being. Clearly expressing your needs can empower your loved ones to provide meaningful support and avoid unintentionally triggering your anxiety.

Encourage open dialogue by inviting questions and addressing any concerns your loved ones may have. Be patient and understanding, recognizing that they may not fully comprehend the complexity of health anxiety. Provide them with educational resources or invite them to join you in therapy sessions to gain a deeper understanding of your experiences.

Remember, effective communication is a two-way street. As you share your experiences, also make an effort to listen to your loved ones. They may have questions, concerns, or their own perspectives to share. By fostering open communication, you can build a support system that is rooted in trust, understanding, and mutual support.

By communicating with your loved ones about your health anxiety, you are inviting them to be part of your journey. Their support and understanding can provide a sense of comfort and strength as you work towards overcoming health anxiety. Embrace open and honest conversations, knowing that your loved ones can be powerful allies in your healing process.

Write a letter to a loved one describing your health anxiety journey, including your feelings, experiences, and challenges. Describe specific fears and worries that you face and how they affect your thoughts and behaviors.

Write a list of specific needs and boundaries you have in relation to your health anxiety. Describe how your loved ones can best support you during challenging times. Be clear about the kind of responses, words, or actions that are helpful and comforting to you.

_____
_____
_____
_____
_____
_____
_____
_____
_____
_____
_____
_____
_____
_____
_____
_____
_____
_____
_____
_____
_____
_____
_____
_____
_____
_____
_____
_____
_____
_____
_____
_____
_____

Reflect on potential questions or concerns that your loved ones may have about your health anxiety. Write down those questions or concerns and prepare thoughtful responses to each one. Consider different perspectives and emotions that your loved ones may bring to the conversation.

Set Achievable Goals

Setting realistic health goals is an important step in overcoming health anxiety. By establishing achievable goals, you can create a sense of direction and purpose on your journey towards managing and reducing anxiety. In this section, we will explore the significance of setting realistic goals and how they can contribute to your progress.

When setting health goals related to your anxiety, it's essential to be mindful of making them attainable and specific. Start by identifying the areas you would like to focus on and the changes you would like to make. These goals can range from reducing the frequency of anxiety symptoms to improving your ability to cope with triggers and stressors. Remember, the purpose of these goals is to support your well-being and provide a roadmap for progress.

Break your goals down into smaller, manageable steps. This approach allows you to work on one aspect at a time, making your goals more achievable. For example, if your goal is to reduce anxiety symptoms, you can start by incorporating relaxation techniques into your daily routine, practicing deep breathing exercises, or engaging in regular physical activity. By taking small steps, you can gradually build momentum and create lasting change.

Consider setting goals that are within your control. While you can't control every aspect of your health or eliminate all anxiety, you can focus on developing healthy coping mechanisms, practicing self-care, and engaging in activities that promote relaxation and well-being. By setting goals that align with your personal agency, you empower yourself to take charge of your health and anxiety management.

Lastly, be kind and patient with yourself as you work towards your goals. Recognize that progress may not always be linear, and setbacks are a natural part of the journey. Celebrate small victories along the way, as these milestones signify progress and growth. Embrace a compassionate mindset and acknowledge the effort and dedication you put into your goals.

Reflect on the areas of your life that are most affected by health anxiety. Reflect on your motivations for setting these goals and why they are important to you personally.

_____
_____
_____
_____
_____

Choose one specific area you identified in the previous exercise to focus on. Write down a specific and measurable goal related to that area. For example, if you want to improve your ability to cope with triggers, a specific goal could be: "Practice a relaxation technique for 10 minutes every day when triggered." Break down your goal into smaller, manageable steps. Write down actionable steps that will help you progress towards your goal. Reflect on how each step is realistic and attainable within your current circumstances.

Write down specific instances or milestones where you noticed positive changes or improvements. Reflect on how these achievements made you feel and how they contributed to your overall well-being.

Write down self-affirmations or positive statements to encourage yourself and boost your confidence in continuing to work towards your goals.

Tracking Progress and Celebrating Milestones

Tracking your progress and celebrating milestones are essential components of goal setting and overcoming health anxiety. These practices provide motivation, reinforcement, and a sense of accomplishment on your journey towards managing anxiety effectively. In this section, we will explore the importance of tracking progress and celebrating milestones, and how they can enhance your overall well-being.

Tracking your progress allows you to observe and reflect on the steps you have taken towards your goals. It provides a visual representation of your efforts, showing how far you have come. Consider using a journal, a progress tracker, or a mobile app to record your achievements, challenges, and the strategies you have implemented. This record will help you identify patterns, evaluate the effectiveness of certain techniques, and adjust your approach as needed.

Regularly reviewing your progress also allows you to celebrate milestones along the way. Milestones can be significant achievements or breakthroughs that mark important progress in managing your health anxiety. For example, it could be successfully applying a new coping mechanism during a challenging situation, completing a therapy session, or going through a medical appointment with reduced anxiety. Recognizing and celebrating these milestones is crucial to staying motivated and reinforcing positive changes.

When celebrating milestones, find ways that resonate with you personally. It could be treating yourself to something you enjoy, practicing self-care, or sharing your accomplishments with your support system. The key is to acknowledge and appreciate the progress you have made. Celebrations not only provide a sense of accomplishment, but they also reinforce the belief in your ability to overcome health anxiety.

Developing a Comprehensive Plan for Maintaining Overall Well-being

Creating a wellness action plan is an important step in overcoming health anxiety and maintaining overall well-being. A comprehensive plan allows you to take a proactive approach to managing your health, both physically and mentally. In this section, we will explore the significance of developing a wellness action plan and how it can support your journey towards a healthier and more balanced life.

Start by reflecting on the different aspects of your well-being: physical, emotional, mental, and social. Consider the activities, practices, and behaviors that contribute to your overall well-being in each of these areas. This may include exercise, healthy eating, adequate sleep, engaging in hobbies, maintaining positive relationships, and seeking emotional support when needed. By identifying these components, you can create a well-rounded plan that addresses your holistic health.

Once you have identified the areas you want to focus on, set specific and achievable goals within each domain of well-being. For example, your goals may include exercising for a certain amount of time each week, practicing relaxation techniques daily, or dedicating time for self-reflection and self-care. Make sure your goals align with your current abilities and resources, allowing for gradual progress.

Consider the resources and support available to you in achieving your wellness goals. This may involve scheduling regular check-ins with a healthcare provider, seeking guidance from a therapist or counselor, or joining support groups that focus on overall well-being. Engaging with these resources provides accountability, guidance, and encouragement as you work towards your goals.

Implement a structured plan by creating a schedule or a daily/weekly routine that incorporates the activities and practices supporting your well-being goals. Be intentional in carving out time for self-care, physical activity, relaxation, and nurturing relationships. Remember, consistency is key in maintaining overall well-being.

Review and adjust your wellness action plan periodically. As you progress, you may find certain strategies are more effective than others or that your needs and circumstances change. Flexibility allows you to adapt and refine your plan to ensure it remains aligned with your current well-being goals.

Identifying Warning Signs and Implementing Coping Strategies

When managing health anxiety, it is important to be aware of warning signs and have coping strategies in place. Identifying these signs can help you recognize when anxiety levels are increasing, enabling you to intervene and implement effective coping mechanisms. In this section, we will explore the significance of identifying warning signs and implementing coping strategies to support your overall well-being.

Start by paying attention to your body and mind. Take note of any physical or emotional changes that often precede or accompany heightened anxiety. These warning signs can vary from person to person and may include increased heart rate, muscle tension, intrusive thoughts, excessive worry, or changes in sleep patterns. By recognizing these signs, you can intervene early and prevent anxiety from escalating.

Once you have identified your warning signs, develop a repertoire of coping strategies that work best for you. These strategies should help you manage and reduce anxiety effectively. Examples include deep breathing exercises, mindfulness or meditation practices, engaging in physical activity, journaling, seeking social support, or engaging in creative outlets. Experiment with different techniques and discover what resonates with you and brings relief.

Create a personalized toolbox of coping strategies that you can access when needed. This toolbox should contain a variety of techniques that address different aspects of well-being—physical, emotional, mental, and social. Keep your toolbox readily available, whether it's a physical box with reminder cards or a digital collection of resources on your phone or computer. This way, you can easily access the coping strategies that work best for you when you encounter warning signs.

Incorporate these coping strategies into your daily routine or wellness action plan. Integrate them as regular practices to promote overall well-being and resilience. By implementing coping strategies consistently, you reinforce healthy habits and build resilience to manage health anxiety effectively.

Create a written schedule or routine that outlines how you will incorporate activities and practices that support your well-being goals. Allocate time for exercise, self-care, relaxation, socializing, and any other activities that promote your overall well-being. Be realistic and consider your existing commitments, then adjust as necessary.

Regularly review your wellness action plan and reflect on your progress. Write about the strategies and activities that have been effective in supporting your well-being and note any challenges or obstacles you've encountered. Make adjustments as needed to ensure your plan remains aligned with your evolving goals and circumstances.

Congratulations on completing the "Embracing Wellness: A Personal Workbook for Overcoming Health Anxiety"!

Throughout this workbook, you have embarked on a transformative journey towards managing and overcoming health anxiety. Let's take a moment to recap the key strategies and tools you have learned to support your ongoing growth and well-being.

In Section 1, you gained a deeper understanding of health anxiety, its symptoms, and its impact on your life. You explored your own health anxiety levels, identified triggers and patterns, and were inspired by real-life stories of individuals who have successfully overcome health anxiety.

Section 2 empowered you to change thought patterns and challenge cognitive distortions associated with health anxiety. By reframing negative thoughts and developing rational thinking, you discovered the power of self-talk and positive affirmations in reshaping your mindset.

Managing anxiety and stress became a priority in Section 3. You explored relaxation techniques, such as breathing exercises and mindfulness, to find moments of calm and restore balance. Coping with uncertainty and developing a balanced approach to seeking medical advice equipped you with the tools to navigate health-related situations with greater confidence.

Section 4 focused on taking control of your health anxiety. By building a support system, you identified sources of support among friends, family, and professionals. Effective communication with your loved ones about your health anxiety fostered understanding and strengthened your relationships. Setting realistic health goals and creating a comprehensive wellness action plan allowed you to maintain overall well-being while tracking progress and celebrating milestones along the way.

As you conclude this workbook, remember that this is not the end of your journey. Continue to embrace the strategies and tools you have learned, adapting them to your evolving needs and circumstances. Be patient and compassionate with yourself as you navigate the ups and downs of managing health anxiety. You are capable of making positive changes and leading a fulfilling life beyond the constraints of anxiety.

In addition to the skills you have developed in this workbook, there are additional resources available to further support your progress. Consider seeking out books, online communities, or local support groups dedicated to anxiety and mental health. Professional guidance from therapists, counselors, or coaches specialized in anxiety can provide ongoing support tailored to your specific needs.

Remember, you are not alone on this journey. Many others have successfully overcome health anxiety, and you can too. Believe in your resilience, inner strength, and capacity for growth. Embrace the power of self-care, self-reflection, and self-compassion as you continue to prioritize your well-being.

Once again, congratulations on completing this workbook. You have taken an important step towards reclaiming control over your health anxiety. May your journey be filled with growth, resilience, and a renewed sense of well-being. Embrace your potential and live a life free from the limitations of anxiety. You have the power to embrace wellness and thrive!

Made in the USA
Monee, IL
14 November 2023